# A Wo
# Microorganisms

by Peter McDonnell

## Table of Contents

Chapter 1

# Microorganisms Everywhere

Did you know that there are tiny living things sitting on you right now? They are on your skin, in your nose, in your mouth, and on your hair. These living things are called **microorganisms**. Microorganisms are also in food, water, and air. They are all around you. Yet you cannot see them without a microscope.

**The photos of microorganisms in this book were taken with a special microscope.**

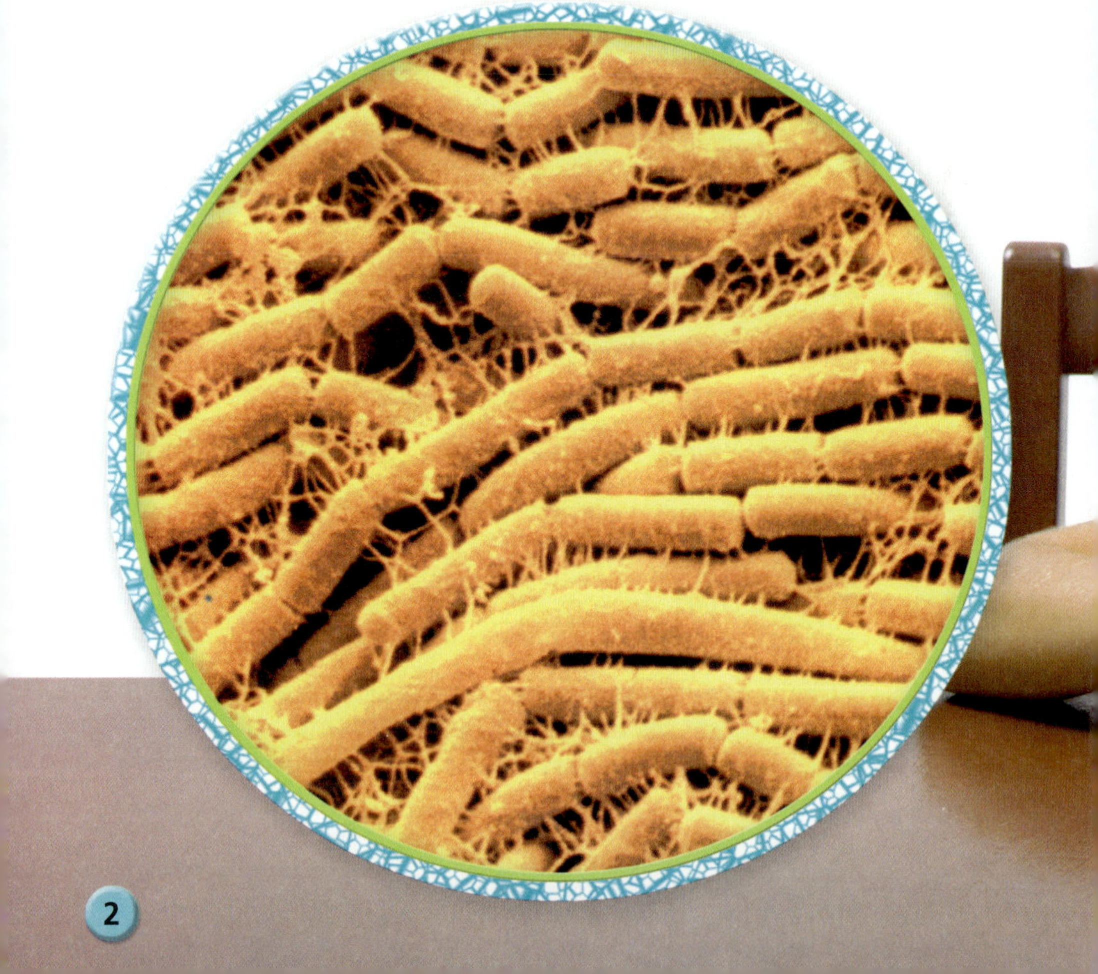

Don't worry! Even though some microorganisms can make people sick, many others can make them well. In fact, microorganisms help people to live. No one could survive without them. In this book, you will learn about different kinds of microorganisms. You will also learn where they live and why people need them.

Microorganisms are some of the smallest living things on Earth. Some are made of only one **cell**. A cell is the smallest unit of living matter. All microorganisms need water to live. Yet they need less than a single millimeter (0.04 inches) of water. A millimeter is about as thick as a fingernail. Because they need so little water, microorganisms can live in soil, in our bodies, and in our food. Some microorganisms can even live in snow or in boiling hot springs.

Microorganisms come in many different shapes. They can be round, long and stringy, or short and fat. They can be corkscrew-shaped or shaped like a blob. There are many different kinds of microorganisms. One gram (0.04 ounces) of soil can contain more than one billion microorganisms.

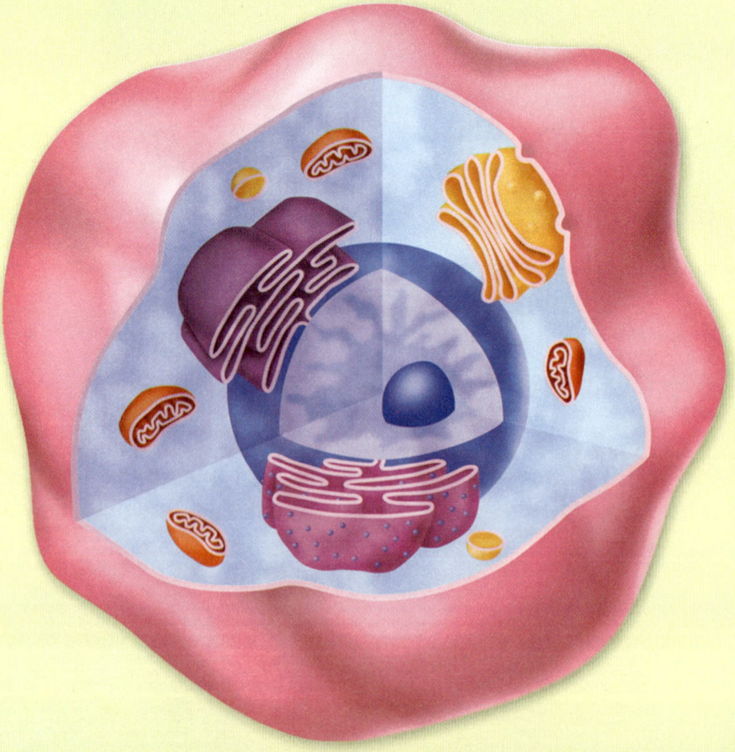

A single animal cell has many parts. Microorganisms are often made of a single cell.

There are probably more microorganisms in this soil than there are people on Earth!

Chapter 2

# Microbes in Your Body

Animals are warm, wet, and full of food for microorganisms. The microorganisms that live on or in animals are called **microbes**. Think of yourself as a hotel for billions of microbes. You have more of them in your body than you have human cells.

When most people think of microbes, they think of disease. Microbes called **bacteria** and **viruses** can cause sickness. But most microbes are not harmful. They help you to live.

Let's start with your skin. Good microbes on your skin keep bad microbes from growing there. You help the good microbes by washing your hands and skin often. Washing keeps harmful microbes from building up and causing infection.

When you are clean, your skin is drier. It is not a good place for microbes to live. When your skin gets sweaty and greasy, it becomes a great home for microbes. The body often smells bad when it is sweaty. This is partly because microbes produce bad-smelling gases.

Microbes live on your skin.

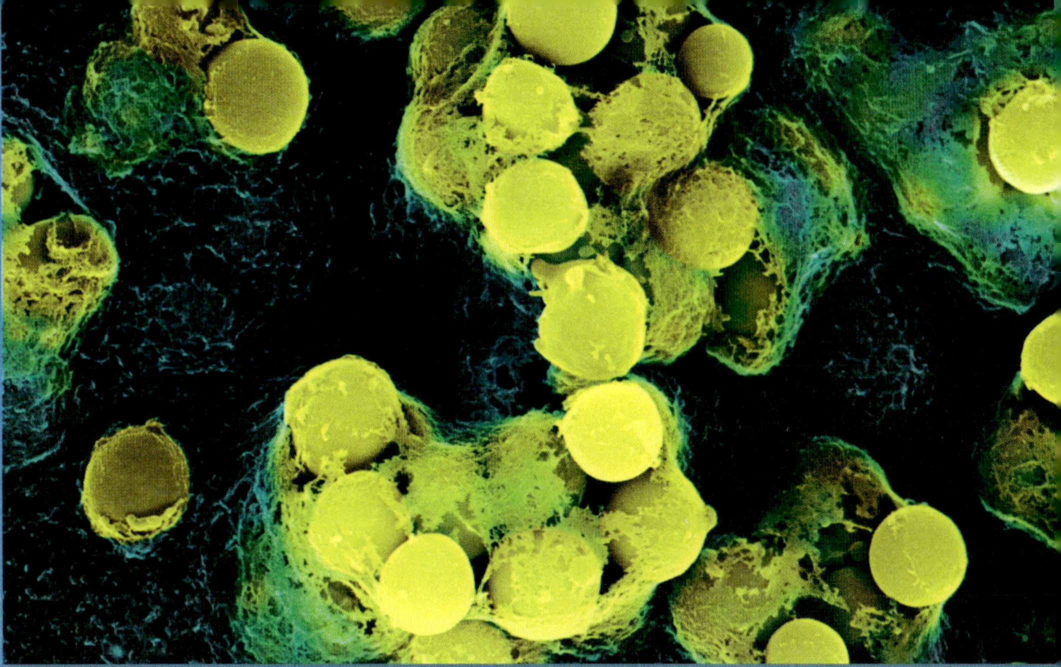

One of many kinds of bacteria

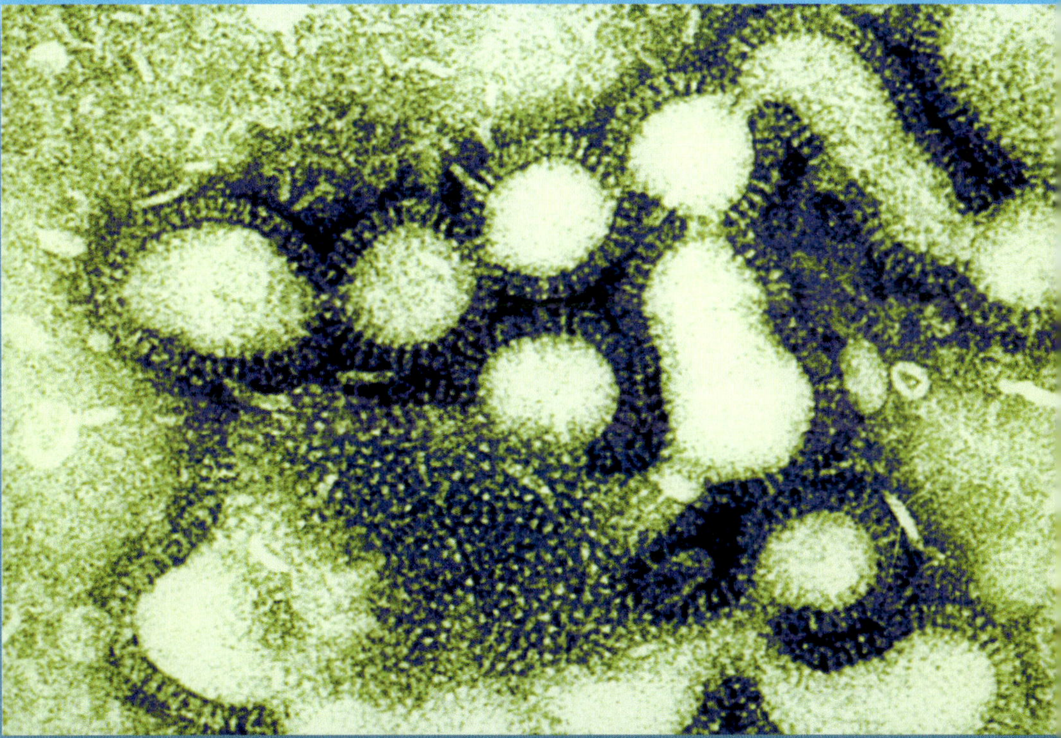

One of many kinds of viruses

Most of the microbes in your body live in your intestine. Your intestine is long and coiled. After food breaks down in your stomach, it passes into your intestine. There, trillions of microbes help break down the food. As you feed yourself, you also feed these microbes.

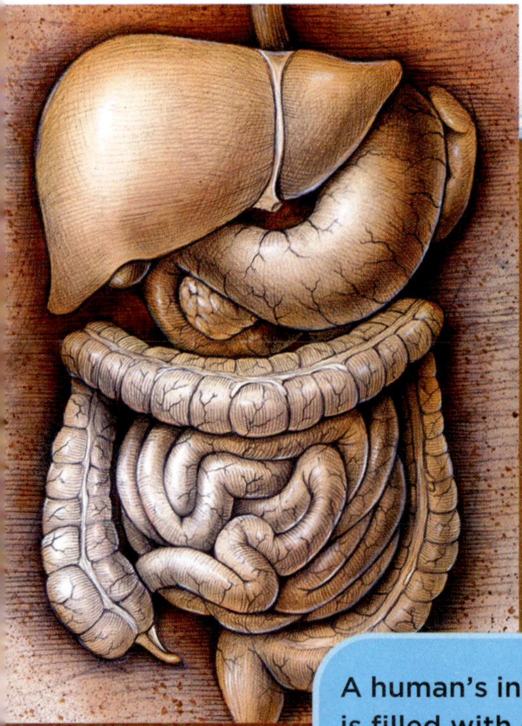

A human's intestine is filled with good microbes.

Some microbes in your intestine make important nutrients that help you to live. *E. coli* makes vitamin K and some B vitamins. Vitamin K helps your blood clot, or get thick, when you have a cut. B vitamins help you turn food into energy. Other microbes in your intestine keep bad microbes from growing.

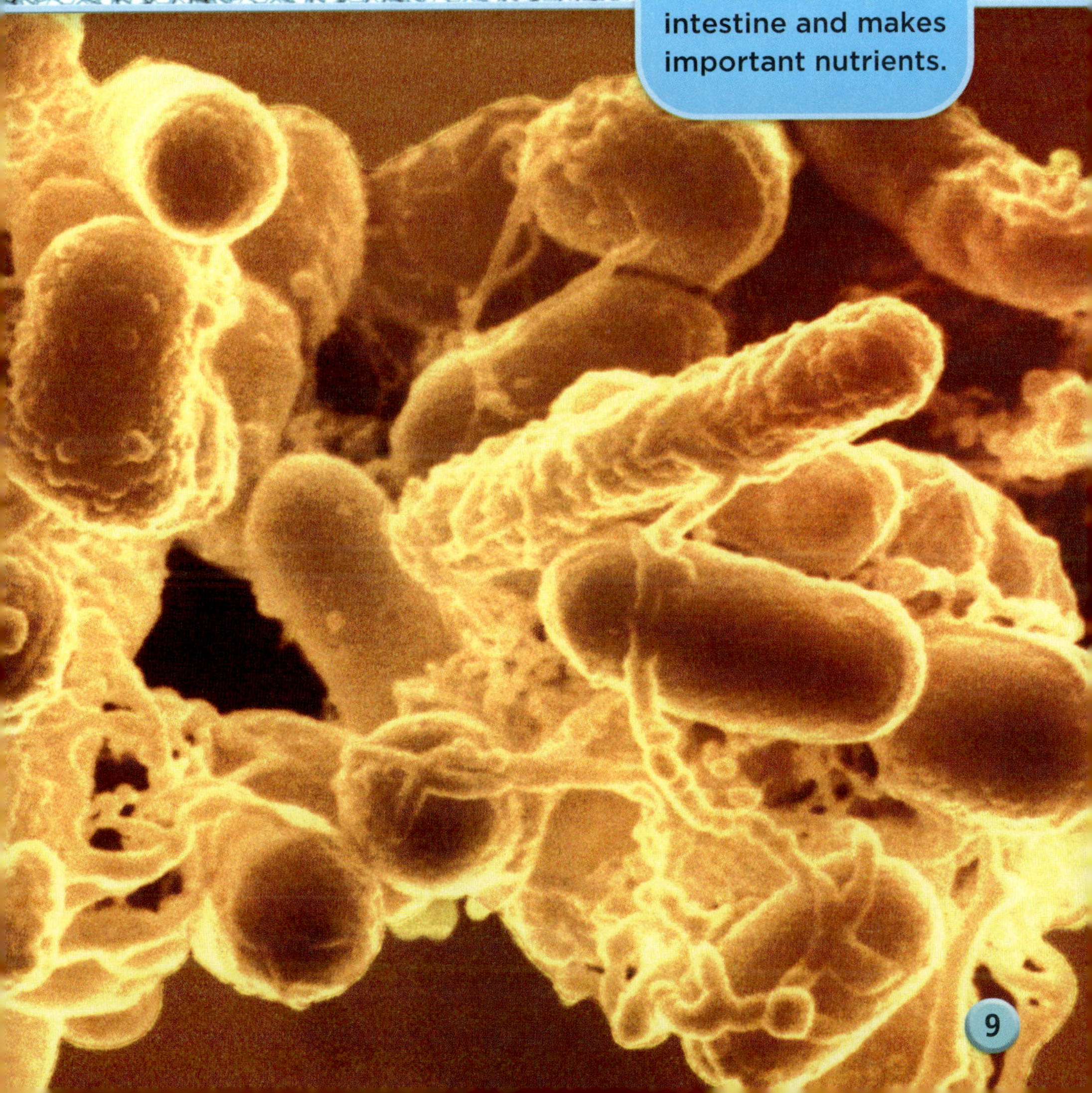

*E. coli* lives in your intestine and makes important nutrients.

Another place where microbes live is in your mouth. That is why you need to brush and floss your teeth, and visit your dentist.

Suppose you take a bite of a candy bar. Microbes in your mouth use the sugar to make an acid that can harm your teeth. Microbes also form a yellowish substance called plaque. This sticks to your teeth and can cause cavities. If you do not brush your teeth, the plaque hardens and can lead to gum disease.

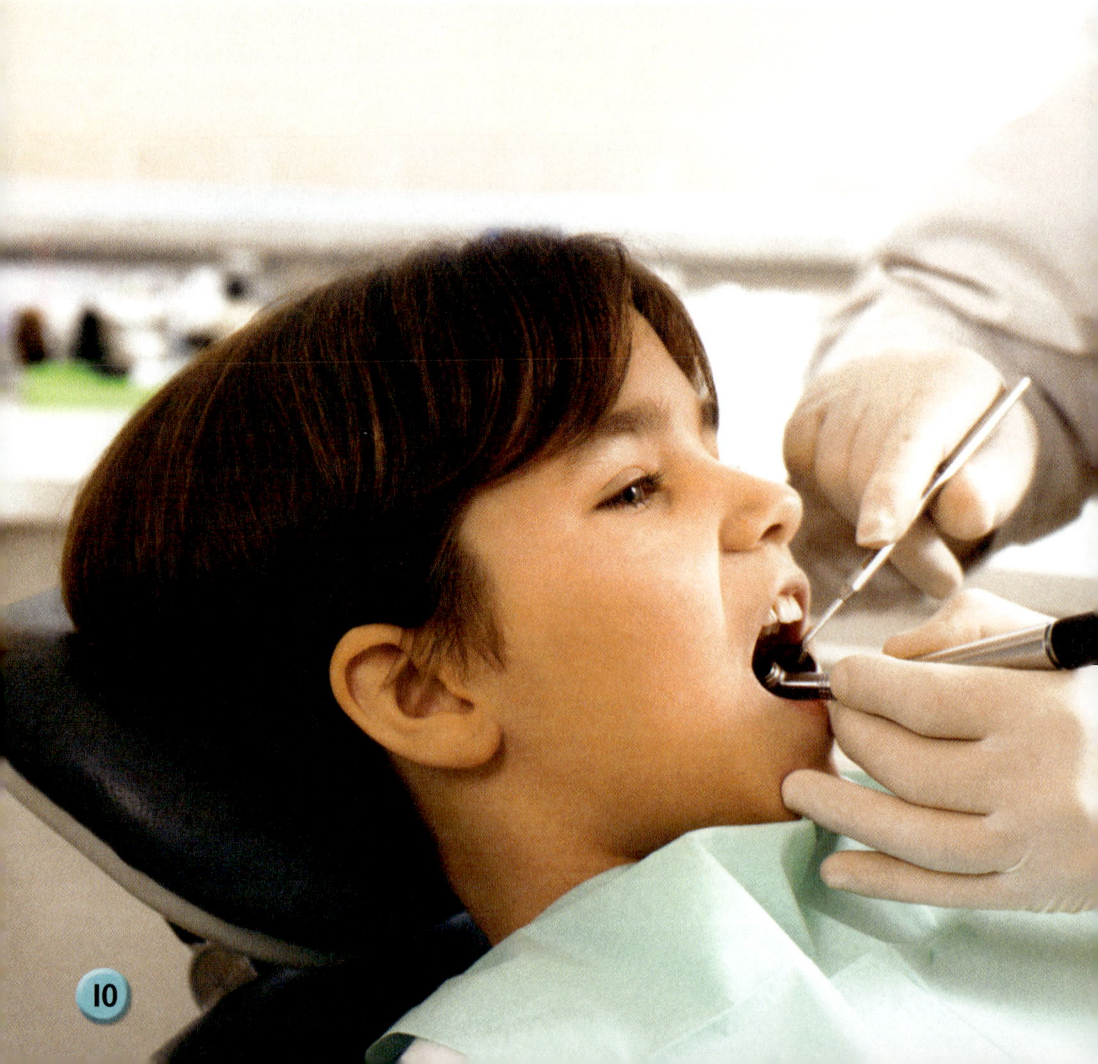

Do you want proof that sugar causes microbes to grow on your teeth? Then try this: Find an old tooth, such as a baby tooth that has fallen out. Drop it into a glass of soda. Make sure the soda is not sugar-free. Leave it there for a few weeks. Check on it every so often. Do you see the tooth decaying? Can you feel it softening? Microbes cause this to happen.

*Streptococcus mutans* is the most common microbe in your mouth. It can cause cavities.

Chapter 3

# Vaccines

Some microbes that were once harmful can be made to become helpful. This is how **vaccines** work.

A vaccine can keep you from getting a disease. Vaccines are made from killed microbes or the parts of microbes that cannot hurt you. A doctor injects a vaccine into your body. If you later become exposed to the real thing, your body will recognize it and prevent it from making you sick. Vaccines have protected you from diseases that used to harm millions of people. We have vaccines for polio, smallpox, measles, and other diseases.

Which vaccines have you had?

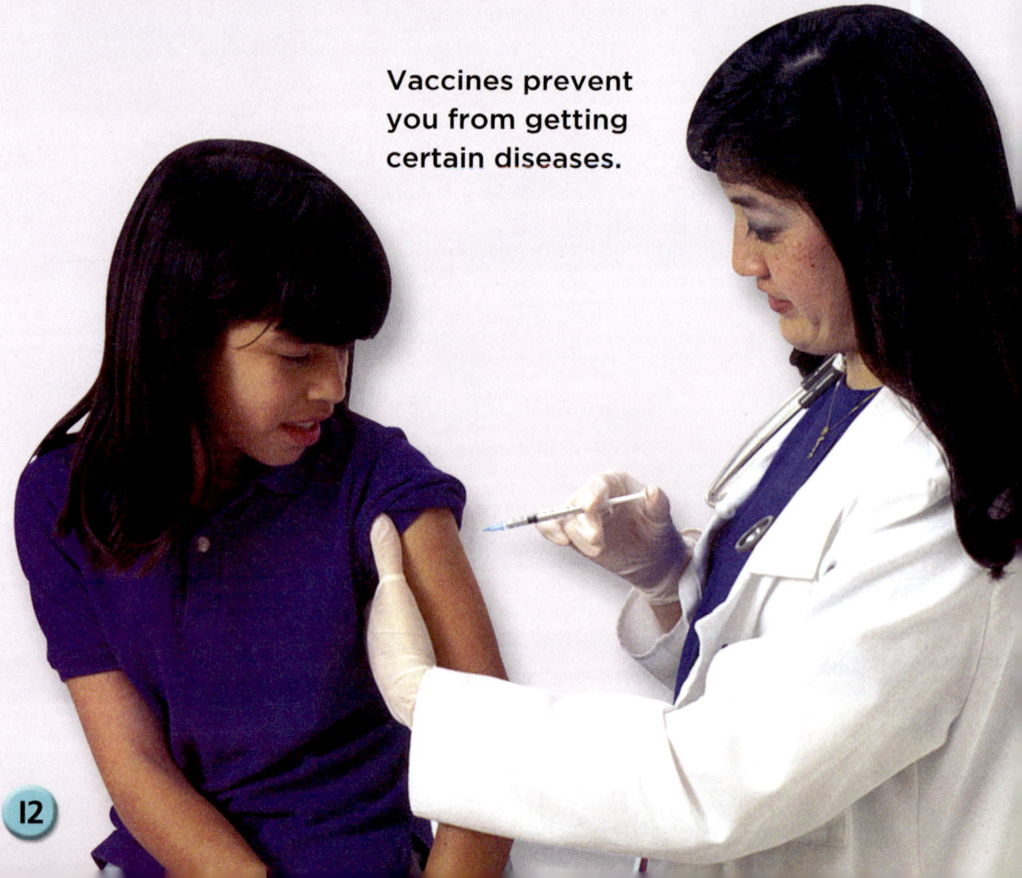

Vaccines prevent you from getting certain diseases.

Franklin Delano Roosevelt, the thirty-second President of the United States, had polio. The disease made him unable to walk. In 1955, Jonas Salk discovered a polio vaccine.

Chapter 4

# Microbes in Your Food

Did you know that cheese, chocolate, and bread are made with microbes? Microbes are also used to make beer, wine, and yogurt. This is done through a process called fermentation. During fermentation, microbes break down the sugars in the liquids. They do this by eating the sugar. In yogurt, the microbe *Lactobacillus* turns milk slightly sour. This microbe also protects the yogurt from other microbes that can make it go bad.

**The microbe *Lactobacillus* turns milk into yogurt.**

Many kinds of bread are made with the help of yeast. Yeast is a microbe. It is a type of fungus. When mixed with flour and warm water, yeast eats the sugars in the flour. It produces carbon dioxide. This gas makes the dough rise. When you knead dough, you give the yeast oxygen. When the yeast takes in the oxygen, the dough rises even more.

Chapter 5

# Microorganisms in the Water

Thousands of different microorganisms live in ponds, oceans, hot springs, and swamps. Ponds are filled with microorganisms. Greenish microorganisms, such as **algae**, live on the top of ponds. This area gets the most sunlight and oxygen. Algae use the sunlight, oxygen, and water to make their food. This is done through **photosynthesis**.

Other microorganisms live deeper in the pond. These microorganisms are darker green or purple. They need less oxygen and sunlight. At the bottom of the pond it is completely dark. There is little oxygen there.

One microorganism found in ponds is the **amoeba**. Unlike other microorganisms, the amoeba cannot make its own food. It must eat other microorganisms. The amoeba looks like a blob. It changes its shape to surround the microorganism it is going to eat. It uses its "feet" to move.

An amoeba lives in water.
It has no set shape.

This one-celled algae is called a diatom. Diatoms can be found in ponds and in soil. Some, like this one, are round. Others are long. There may be more than 10,000 species of diatoms.

Many kinds of microorganisms live in this hot spring.

Microorganisms also live in the salty ocean. There are more plants, animals, and microorganisms living in the ocean than on land. Most microorganisms live at the top of the ocean. This is where there is sunlight. Below 23 meters (75 feet), the ocean is very dark. Fewer animals and plants can survive there.

It is impossible to count the number of microorganisms living in the ocean.

Deep down in the ocean, there is no light. The water is very cold. Yet the ocean floor has hydrothermal vents. These vents give off hot air and a gas. Microorganisms live inside worms that grow around these vents. These microorganisms make food for the worms. This is an example of **symbiosis**. In symbiosis, living things depend on each other to live.

At the bottom of the ocean, microorganisms live inside worms. These worms live around hydrothermal vents.

Chapter 6

# Microorganisms in the Soil

Microorganisms that live in the soil eat almost anything organic. When something is organic, it comes from a living organism. Microorganisms will eat banana peels, leaves, pine needles, and grass. When they eat a pile of leaves, they break down the leaves and turn them into soil. This soil is filled with nutrients. Many people make **compost** piles out of leaves, table scraps, and garden waste. They do it to cut down on garbage. They also do it to make soil for their gardens.

In farming, some microorganisms cause problems. Others solve problems. Certain kinds of microorganisms ruin crops. They make plants rot and die. Other kinds fill the soil with nutrients. Today, farmers use microorganisms to keep harmful insects away from crops. They do this to keep their crops healthy. Insecticides made from chemicals can hurt the environment. Insecticides made from microorganisms are less harmful.

Compost pile

This person is making a compost pile.

Another way that microorganisms help keep the environment healthy is by breaking down harmful chemicals. In many places around the world, these chemicals pollute the land and water. They are poisonous. They hurt humans, other animals, and plants. It is lucky that there are microorganisms that can grow in these chemicals. They break down these chemicals into harmless substances.

The microorganisms in our land, water, food, and bodies make life possible. We could not live without them.

# Glossary

**algae** (AL-jee) *pl. n., sing.* **alga** (AL-guh) tiny one-celled organisms *(page 16)*

**amoeba** (uh-MEE-buh) a one-celled microorganism found in water *(page 16)*

**bacteria** (bak-TEER-ee-uh) *pl. n., sing.* **bacterium** [bak-TEER-ee-um]) a one-celled microbe *(page 6)*

**cell** (SEL) the smallest unit of living matter *(page 4)*

**compost** (KOM-pohst) a mixture of decaying organic materials used to nourish soil *(page 20)*

**microbe** (MIGH-krohb) a very tiny organism, usually, a bacterium or a virus *(page 6)*

**microorganism** (migh-kroh-OR-guh-niz-uhm) a living thing so small you need a microscope to see it *(page 2)*

**photosynthesis** (foh-tuh-SIN-thuh-sis) a process in plants that uses energy from sunlight to make food from water and carbon dioxide *(page 16)*

**symbiosis** (sim-bee-OH-sis) a relationship between two kinds of organisms that depend on each other *(page 19)*

**vaccine** (vak-SEEN) a substance made of the dead or weakened microbes of a certain disease to help the body protect itself from that disease *(page 12)*

**virus** (VIGH-ruhs) a simple microbe that can multiply in living cells and cause many diseases *(page 6)*

# Index